The Biblical Foundation
for the
Military Profession

The Biblical Foundation for the Military Profession

Is the Christian faith compatible with the military profession?

Can a Christian be a soldier?

Clay Buckingham
Major General,
United States Army (retired)

The Biblical Foundation for the Military
Profession

By Clay T. Buckingham

Copyright © 2022 by Clay T. Buckingham

Published by Risky Living Ministries, Inc.
www.RLMIN.com

ISBN: 9798806296710

Written to encourage logical, analytical thinking about the legitimacy and purpose of the military profession from the biblical viewpoint.

The Biblical Foundation for the Military Profession

—Is the Christian faith compatible with the military profession?
—Can a Christian be a soldier?

"I'm a Marine. I can't be a Christian."

The combat decorated colonel continued: "The Bible says, *'Thou shalt not kill.'* And killing is required in my profession."

Case closed.

Hmmm?

"We are resigning our commissions."

The two young Air Force captains, both fighter pilots, had committed their lives to Jesus at a church service a few months earlier.

Now they faced a dilemma.

Is the military profession compatible with the Christian faith?

They had both been advised that it was not.

"The way of Jesus is the way of peace and turning the other cheek, not the way of war and killing fellow human beings. So the only honorable thing for us to do is to resign our commissions and enter a biblically permitted profession."

End of discussion.

Or is it?

Before going any further, let's unpack the sixth commandment, **"Thou shalt not kill"** (Exodus 20:13 KJV -- The King James Version was first published in 1620).

This one statement, more than any other biblical text, has caused Christians everywhere to question the legitimacy of

the military profession, whether a Christian can be a soldier.

The word *kill* is a broad term. It conveys the meaning of purposely ending the life of something which is alive. Some go so far as to apply the meaning to animals or even plants, to anything with life.

The broadly accepted assumption is that the sixth commandment applies to ending the life of a fellow human being.

Does this mean that the Bible prohibits the killing of another human being in all circumstances?

The authors of the KJV broadly translated the original Hebrew word in the source documents as **kill**.

Later translators refined the term to **murder** using source documents not available to the KJV translators in 1620.

In the New International Version (NIV), Copyright 1978, New York International

Bible Society, Exodus 20:13 reads, "You shall not **murder**."

In the NKJV (New King James Version), Copyright 1982, Thomas Nelson, the reference reads, "You shall not **murder**."

In the Sermon on the Mount, Jesus refers to the Ten Commandments when He states, "You have heard that it was said to people long ago, 'Do not **murder**'" (Matthew 5:21 NIV) or "You shall not **murder**" (same reference, NKJV).

Murder is a much more precise and limited word than **kill**.

Here is a dictionary definition of **murder** from *Webster's New World Dictionary of the American Language*, Encyclopedic Edition, P. F. Collier and Son, New York.

Murder is: *"The unlawful and malicious or premeditated killing of one human being by another."*

Almost everyone, everywhere would agree that murder is wrong.

Every civilized society has laws prohibiting murder.

But most civilized societies also have laws that authorize the killing of another human being under certain circumstances.

An individual citizen may, in self-defense, legally kill an attacker coming at him with a butcher knife in his bedroom.

A policeman may legally kill an active shooter in a schoolhouse to save the lives of students.

Soldiers may legally kill opposing soldiers of an invading force to protect the lives of the citizens of their country.

Augustine concluded that killing to protect the defenseless or innocent was biblically lawful. Christian theologians later expanded this concept to include self-defense. The Just War Theory, based on the belief that self-defense extended to nations, eventually became widely accepted by Christians, hundreds of years *before* the sixth commandment was translated in the KJV as "Thou shalt not kill."

But the inaccurate interpretation persists, and many Christians still seriously but erroneously take the 400-year-old KJV translation at its face value. They fail to realize that the original biblical statement declares, "Thou shall not **murder**."

To Proceed

**Is the military profession compatible with the Christian faith?
Can a Christian be a soldier?**

In order to answer this question, we need to compare:

+ *What the Bible teaches about Christian conduct and responsibility*

with

+ The fundamental purpose of the military profession.

First,

What does the Bible teach about Christian conduct and responsibility?

According to an old catechism, the Bible is the "all-sufficient guide to faith and practice."

+ What should I believe (faith)? Read the Bible and find out.

+ How should I live (practice)? Read the Bible and find out.

You need not go anywhere else. As a Christian, the Bible is **your** *all-sufficient guide for faith and practice.*

As a believer and follower of Jesus, **How should I live? What should I do? What should I not do?**

The answers are in the Bible.

There are two main characters in the Bible: **God and Man.**

Essentially, the Bible teaches us:

What we should **believe** about **God and Man (faith)**

What we should **do** about **God and Man (practice)**

Brief examples:

What should we **believe** about God? - That God created the heavens and the earth. (Genesis 1:1)

What should we **do** about God? - Love the Lord your God with all of your heart, mind and soul. (Matthew 22:37)

What should we **believe** about Man? - That God created man in His own image. (Genesis1:27)

What should we **do** about Man? - Love your neighbor as yourself. (Matthew 22:39)

Throughout the Bible, there are hundreds and hundreds of statements describing:

What we should *believe* about God.
What we should *do* about God.
What we should *believe* about Man.
What we should *do* about Man.

Among many other things, the Bible is a history of God's love and provision for Man.

Man is God's highest creation. He was made in the very image of God. As such, every human life, from conception until natural death, inherently possesses sanctity, honor, dignity, value, worth, importance and inviolability.

After the creation God proclaimed that everything He had created - *including Man* - was good.

How does **God** view **Man** - the work of His own hands?

Here is how it is expressed in Zephaniah 3:17 (NIV):

"The Lord your God is with you.
He is mighty to save [protect].
He takes great delight in you.
He comforts you with His love.
He rejoices over you with singing."

We are His children, His ultimate creation, and He loves us with infinite and everlasting love.

This love is expressed in giving - in providing for our needs. The epitome of his love is recorded in John 3:16:

"For God so **loved** the world that He gave His only begotten Son, that whosoever believes in Him might have eternal life."

How does all of this relate to Christian conduct and responsibility?

Our view of Man should be the same as God's view of Man.

It means that Christians should do everything they can to protect, support, sustain and

enhance the lives of our fellow human beings
- God's ultimate creation.

This is what it means to love our neighbors as
ourselves.

**So what does the Bible teach about
Christian conduct and responsibility?**

The gold standard for conduct as a Christian
can be stated as follows:

**Whatever protects and enhances the lives
of our fellow human beings is good.**

**Whatever destroys or degrades human life
is evil.**

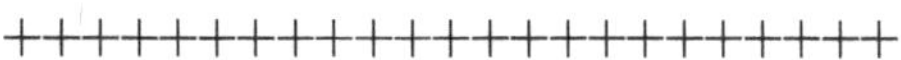

Second,

**What is the fundamental purpose of the
military profession?**

God created the world to provide a place for man to live, work and raise a family in fellowship with Him.

His desire is that the environment where men live should be secure, peaceful, just, orderly and free.

God created three organizations for the structure of His society of men: family, church and civil government.

We will consider civil government only at this time. Family and church are relevant, but not integral for our consideration of the fundamental purpose of the military profession.

The purpose of civil government is to provide the secure, peaceful, just, orderly, and free environment where man can live, work, and raise a family in fellowship with God.

Today the world has almost 200 separate and distinct civil societies. These societies have come to be called nations.

Each nation consists of a land area with people and resources, separate and independent of all other nations. It is an independent political entity having its own civil government with the God-given purpose of providing a secure, peaceful, just, orderly and free environment where man can live, work, raise a family in fellowship with God.

Security comes first. It is the primal responsibility of civil government.

Without **security** there can be no peace, justice, order, or freedom.

What is **security**? It is a state of being where the people within a society may live, work, and raise a family without fear of danger or disruption.

Threats to the security of the people of a nation come in basically two forms: external and internal.

External threats are posed by the military forces of a neighbor nation. The invading military forces of an aggressive, unfriendly neighbor nation pose an imminent threat to the lives, property, and everyday way of life of the citizens of the invaded nation.

Internal threats come from local criminals and terrorists. The lives, property, and way of life of local citizens can de deeply threatened and disrupted by unconstrained local criminals and terrorists.

External threats can only be successfully opposed by superior national military force.

Internal threats can only be met by highly trained and disciplined local police forces.

The military profession is that sub-society within the greater national society which is uniquely set apart to provide for the national defense. No other segment of the larger society has that mission. If a nation has no military profession, it will have no national defense. It will be vulnerable to outside aggression and the citizens of that nation will be forever insecure.

It is a fact of history that we live in a dangerous world. At every stage in recorded history there has been at least one nation (or entity or ethnic group) which has been unprincipled and aggressive.

Looking around the world today, there are at least four such nations - maybe more.

Only the strong, or those allied to the strong, can remain free.

Of the almost 200 nations of the world today, almost every one of them has some kind of military force which has the mission of national defense.

Unfortunately, a significant number of these nations harbors some longstanding grievance against or territorial interest in a neighbor nation but is prevented from taking aggressive military action against the neighbor nation only because of the deterrent effect of the neighbor nation's armed forces and those of its allies.

In today's world the security of our nation (or any nation) and its people can only be maintained by the deterrent effect of our armed forces and the willingness of our government to use those armed forces against any opposing nation which is actively threatening the lives, property, and way of life of our people.

Our Founding Fathers, the writers of our Constitution, stated in the Preamble that one of the six great purposes of the Constitution was to "provide for the common defense." This assumes the establishment and maintenance of military forces.

They also said that another one of the purposes is "to insure domestic tranquility." This assumes the establishment and maintenance of police forces.

The other four purposes of the Constitution are: to form a more perfect union, to establish justice, to promote the general welfare, and to secure the blessings of liberty for ourselves and our posterity.

Military force is neither good nor evil. It is how it is used which gives it moral content.

Military force is good when it is used to defend the nation against outside aggression, thus protecting the lives of the people so that they can live lives in security, peace, justice, order and freedom.

Military force is evil when it is used to attack a peaceful nation and thus destroy the lives and property of its people.

We thus deduce that the fundamental purpose of the military profession is:

To protect the lives of the nation's people against outside aggression so that they live in peace, with justice, order and freedom.

In Sum - -

Earlier we asked:

  *** Is the military profession compatible with the Christian faith?**
  *** Can a Christian be a soldier?**

And then further stated:

 *** In order to answer this question, we need to compare:**

 + What the Bible teaches about Christian conduct and responsibility

with

 + The fundamental purpose of the military profession.

1. The Bible teaches that whatever <u>protects</u> and enhances <u>the lives of</u> our fellow human beings is good.

2. The purpose of the military profession is to <u>protect the lives of</u> our nation's people against outside aggression so that we may live in peace, with justice, order, and freedom.

Comparing these two, we conclude that:

 *** Yes, the military profession is compatible with the Christian faith.**

* Yes, a Christian can be a soldier.

* The key consistency is "... <u>protect the lives of...</u>"

* A Christian soldier can fully participate in all of the legitimate activities of his profession knowing that the military profession is a biblically approved profession.

* However, at all times, soldiers are constrained and guided in their conduct by the values and ethics promulgated by their particular service (Army, Navy, Air Force, Marines, Coast Guard). In wartime, all soldiers are guided in their conduct by the Geneva Convention and the Code of Conduct of their service.

Addendum

Some Additional Thoughts:

 * The proper use of military force (and police force) is consistent with the most noble teaching of the Bible about Man - the sanctity and dignity of human life.

 * The Bible supports the use of military force only when it is used legitimately, (i.e., defending the lives, the property, and way of life of the people of our nation.)

 * A major function of military force is deterrence—to preserve peace through strength—not to promote war.

 * In the Bible, references to soldiering are generally positive. Soldiering is viewed as a common, normal, understood, accepted profession.

 * The Apostle Paul uses examples of soldiering several times to explain elements of the Christian faith.

  * Jesus commends a Roman **soldier** for his **faith**. This, in itself, confirms the compatibility of the Christian faith with the military profession.

++++++++++++++++++++++++++++

Ending footnote: This analysis of the compatibility of the Christian faith with the military profession is only the beginning of the discussion, but the conclusions stated herein comprise the essential foundation for future discussions on **when** we should fight and **how** we should fight.

About the Author

Clay Buckingham was born in Vero Beach, Florida. One of five children, he was raised in a family where education, integrity, and hard work were core values and where service to God, country, and community were exampled and expected. His father, a successful citrus grower, served in France during WWII as an infantry lieutenant.

Buckingham entered the United States Military Academy at West Point, NY, at age 18. He was invited to attend a cadet Bible study, and it was through this experience that he committed his life to Jesus Christ. During his senior year, he joined a fledgling organization called the Officers' Christian Fellowship (OCF). He graduated from West Point in June 1949 and was commissioned as a U.S. Army lieutenant.

Buckingham served as a tank platoon leader and company commander in combat during the Korean War. As a lieutenant colonel, he served as an advisor to South Vietnamese Army Forces during the Vietnam War. During his career, Buckingham commanded four companies, an armored cavalry squadron, and an armored brigade. He also served as an armored division chief of staff, assistant division commander, and finally commander of the U.S. Army Computer Systems Command. He retired in 1982 as a major general.

In November 1952, Clay married Clara Jean Miller, a native of Texas and a graduate of Baylor University. God has blessed them with four children, 21 grandchildren, and 34 great grandchildren.

After retirement from the Army, Clay and Clara moved to Pennsylvania, where they have worked as volunteers at White Sulphur Springs, the Eastern Conference and Retreat Center of the OCF. They have also been active volunteers with the Association of Military Fellowships (AMCF), the Association for Christian Conferences, Teaching, and Service (ACCTS), and the International Association of Evangelical Chaplains (IAEC).